Adventures at
CAMP POOTIE-CHO

Sapo for President

Written by Ophelia S. Lewis

Illustrated by Shabamukama Osbert

VILLAGE TALES PUBLISHING
LAWRENCEVILLE, GA

A Sapo Children's Book
Published by Village Tales Publishing
Text Copyright ©2020 by Ophelia S. Lewis
Illustrations copyright ©2020 Village Tales Publishing

All rights reserved. No part of this book may be reproduced, or transmitted in any form of electronic or mechanical, including photocopying, recording, or by any information storage and retrieval system without written permission from the publisher, except for the inclusion of brief quotation in a review.

A catalog record for this book is available from the Library of Congress:
LCCN: 2020900048
ISBN: 9781945408571

Cover Design By OASS

Dedicated to Liberian children everywhere

www.villagetalespublishing.com
www.oass.villagetalespublishing.com
www.childrens.villagetalespublishing.com

Elections at Camp Pootie-Cho

The campers happily gathered for an assembly to hear the news Mr. Bayogar had promised.

"We are going to have a mock election," Mr. Bayogar announced. "Hopefully, you'll understand how we elect our leaders."

"What's a mock election?" Quama asked, raising her hand.

"You are going to learn how to choose a public leader," Mr. Bayogar answered. "You are going to vote. We will follow the same rules and all the procedures as if we are choosing a real president for Liberia."

"Awesome!" Quama yelled. "I want to be the president."

"A girl can't be president," Jenks said. "The president has to be a boy. Maybe Sapo or Razaq can be the president."

"What about Faaz?" Riah asked. "He's a boy."

"He can't talk with his voice," Jenks said. "He has to use his hands."

"Anyone can be president," Mr. Bayogar said, "even those citizens who speak with signs. Besides, Ellen Johnson-Sirleaf was president. If Faaz wants to be president, he can too."

"I don't want to be president," Faaz signed with his hand.

The Process

"Here are the rules," Mr. Bayogar said. "Since there are fifteen counties, and fifteen campers, each camper will represent a county. Together, you represent Liberia."

"My grandma lives in Ganta, so I want to represent Nimba County," Asatu said.

"That's not the way it's going to work," Mr. Bayogar said. "I have written the name of each county on a piece of paper. Each camper will pick a piece of paper and whatever name you pick is the county you will represent."

Mr. Bayogar asked Ms. Una to help him place the pieces of paper in a hat. The campers grumbled.

"Mind your manners," Mr. Bayogar reminded.

"What if I don't want to represent the county I picked?" Gola asked.

"That's the rule, Gola," Mr. Bayogar said. "Remember your good manners alphabet. O is for, Obey Rules."

Ms. Una carried the hat around until everyone picked a piece of paper. They each announced which county they represented with glee.

Sapo picked Maryland, Gola (Grand Bassa), Bendu (Lofa), Quama (Grand Cape Mount), Quincy (River Cess), Cyrus (Bomi), Faaz (Montserrado), Asatu (Sinoe), Riah (Grand Kru), Solo (Margibi), Lazzie (Gbarpolu), Kweeta (Grand Gedeh), Jenks (River Gee), Nawei (Nimba), and Razaq picked Bong County.

"We will have two teams," Mr. Bayogar said. "Your team is also called your party. One party will be named One-for-all, and the other will be called, All-for-one. Learn everything about the candidates and their ideas. The candidates will debate on why their idea is better."

"What's a candidate and a debate?" Quama asked.

"A candidate is someone who wants your vote, and a debate is when different candidates explain why their idea is the best. Listen to both sides and ask questions. The candidates will answer your questions to help you understand their plans."

"Next, you will choose who you want to become president by using a ballot. The ballot is a card with the candidates' pictures on it. Mark an x on the candidate you choose. That's how you vote. Your vote is your choice. Voting is a good way to be a part of big public decisions. During an election, every vote matters and every vote is counted."

Choosing the Candidates

"We need candidates," Mr. Bayogar said. "You may suggest someone to run for president. You can also volunteer yourself."

"I would like to be president, Mr. Bayogar," Sapo said, raising his hand. "How do I choose who's on my team?"

"You can run for president, Sapo," Mr. Bayogar said, "but you don't choose who's on your team. Each camper will make that choice when they vote, based on what you promise to do if you are elected. That's how it's done in the real election. We are only looking for candidates at this time."

"I would like to be president too," Bendu said. "Can I run?"

"Yes, you can, Bendu," Mr. Bayogar said. "You can be the other candidate. Anyone else?"

No one raised their hand.

"Well, we have the candidates," Mr. Bayogar said. "Sapo will lead the All-for-one party and Bendu will represent One-for-all. The next step is to hear the candidates share their ideas. Tomorrow, they will debate."

The Debate

"It's time to debate," Mr. Bayogar said at the next camp assembly. "Listen to the candidates' ideas and promises. Ask yourself, 'Can they truly do what they promise?'"

Ms. Una handed Bendu and Sapo microphones.

"Bendu will go first," Mr. Bayogar said. "She won the coin toss."

"If I'm elected, I will build a playground," Bendu said. "We need space for activities."

"We don't need a playground because we already have the football field and basketball court," Sapo said. "That's where we all play. If I'm elected, I will get brand new jerseys for the football and basketball teams."

All the athletes clapped happily.

"The football and basketball players are always using

the football field and basketball court," Bendu argued. "So, everyone else has to stop playing earlier than we want to. When we get a playground, everybody will be able to play for as long as they would like. And, the football team can practice for as long as they need."

"We won't be able to show off the playground to anyone outside of Camp Pootie-Cho," Sapo said. "But we can show off our new uniforms when we play other camps in different counties."

"That's right, Sapo," Jenks said, smiling. "I totally agree."

"What about the rest of us?" Lazzie asked.

"We will make you proud," Sapo answered. "We already win most of our games. With new uniforms, we will win all of our games. The cheerleaders will get new uniforms too."

Everyone clapped cheerfully.

"What do you think, Faaz," Quama asked.

"I don't know," Faaz signed. "I'm so confused."

"Me too," Quama replied.

Let's Campaign

During the week, Sapo worked hard to get the campers to join All-for-one and Bendu worked hard to make them join One-for-all.

"I'm more popular than Bendu," Sapo bragged to his teammates. "Everybody likes me."

"They will like you more if you give them treats," Jenks suggested. "Everyone will vote for you."

"Good idea," Sapo said.

All week Sapo handed out cookies and candies, while Bendu talked to each camper, explaining why a playground would be better.

"Why build a playground, Bendu," Kweeta asked. "You can't run or jump around like everybody else?"

"It's not just for me, or the girls," Bendu said.

"Everybody can enjoy the playground. If an adult helps me to get on the swing, I can have fun too. Everyone can have fun all day long."

"I like that idea," Kweeta said.

As Election Day came nearer, Dr. Harris, the camp counselor, talked with the campers about electing the best candidate.

"Choose a good decision-maker," she advised. "A good leader thinks of others and acts on their behalf, rather than only being concerned with his or her own needs."

Hip Hop Hooray, It's Election Day!

The campers patiently stood in a long line to vote. Officer Yeahum handed each camper a ballot card.

"Go inside the booth, mark an x on the candidate you choose, fold the ballot card, and push it into the slot at the top of the box," Officer Yeahum said. "Remember, only one person at a time in the booth."

After explaining, he waved them by. Each voter made their decision as Officer Yeahum had instructed. Everybody voted fairly. Then Mr. Bayogar and Ms. Una counted every ballot card. The results were in!

The Winner is . . .

Campers and staff gathered to hear the winner's name.

"All-for-one and One-for-all did an awesome job," Mr. Bayogar said. "You followed the rules as if this were a real election. Remember to do the same when you are old enough to vote."

Everybody clapped, but not for long. They were all eager to know who'd won the election.

"It was close," Mr. Bayogar announced, "but Bendu won the elections! Eight votes to seven."

Sapo stopped smiling. He really wanted to pout but did not.

"Congratulations, Bendu," he sighed and shook her hand. "Good luck with your project."

"Thank you, Sapo," Bendu said. "We both did a good job. We should work together on the playground project."

Bendu talked to Mr. Gaimuni about the new playground.

"We want a seesaw, a merry-go-round, one tire swing, a slide, a jungle gym, a sandbox, picnic tables, and a playhouse."

"That's a lot of work," Mr. Gaimuni said.

"Everybody will help," Bendu said. "It's always better working together."

"And, fun too," Mr. Gaimuni added.

A Promise Kept

One week later, a big truck delivered supplies for the playground. The truck brought stacks of logs, planks, wheelbarrows and shovels, paint cans, rubber tires, chains, and other materials. Mr. Gaimuni got the team together and assigned each camper a job. He made sure everyone wore safety glasses and hardhats.

Soon, the campers were banging hammers, toting sand in wheelbarrows and buckets, and drilling poles into the ground. They sang too. Chef Chewie served rice bread, sandwiches, and ginger beer drinks.

Trash cans and a water fountain were added to make the playground better.

"Now that the playground is finished, we have to give it a name," Bendu said. "What would you suggest, Sapo?"

Surprised, Sapo asked, "You are the winner, Bendu, shouldn't you give the new playground its name?"

"Building the playground was my idea," Bendu said. "But I think you should name it."

"Really?"

"Yes," Bendu said. "You should name it."

Sapo smiled.

"Let's name it after Oldman Juuku," he suggested. "He works hard to keep Camp Pootie-Cho clean."

"That's a good idea!" Bendu said.

"And, a good way to appreciate and honor him," Mr. Bayogar added. "You children have made me proud."

Time to Play

Juuku Playground became a place for recreation. It also helped the campers develop physical skills. But most importantly, they had voted on it together. All the campers enjoyed playing on the various play equipment. Everyone was happy.

A Message From the Author

Your vote is very important. It is how you choose which community workers should be in charge. A politician is a community worker, like a teacher who takes care of your education, a doctor who cares for you when you are sick, a taxi driver who takes you to the places you need to go, or a market woman who sells you food to eat. A politician works for the community too. A good politician makes sure every citizen gets equally from the country's resources, not just some citizens.

When you are old enough to vote, remember to vote for politicians who build schools, hospitals, bridges, and roads. Vote for politicians who give us safe drinking water, create clean environments, and help farmers grow food. Do NOT vote for politicians who give small gifts like t-shirts or bags of rice in order to get your vote and win the election. Small gifts are good for just you. Big gifts are good for everybody. A good citizen cares about others. Be a good citizen. Be a good politician. Be a good community worker.

Ophelia S. Lewis (Author)

A mission to transform the limited books available with African characters in children's books today, drawing from her own childhood for inspiration, Lewis creates cultural-genre books with African characters all children can relate to. Of her work, Lewis says, "The best way of getting people familiar with the importance of identity and own surroundings is through the eyes of childhood. Start at the earliest stage of life." Learn more about her work at www.ophelialewis.com

Books by Ophelia S. Lewis

A is for Africa * I'm About To * Toby Pannoh's Good Manners for Boys and Girls * GMA (how to be a super polite kid) * Where in the World is Liberia * Aventures at Camp Pootie-Cho Game & Puzzle Activity Book * Keeping Secrets

Shabamukama Osbert (Illustrator)

Since joining Village Tales Publishing in 2016, Osbert has done illustrations for several books by different authors; BALLAH MAKES SHAPES (Augustus Y. Voahn), TOBY PANNOH'S GOOD MANNERS FOR BOYS AND GIRLS (Ophelia S. Lewis), LITTLE BRAVE LYDIA and DRAMA ON PIPELINE ROAD (Nemen M. Kpahn), BETTER TOGETHER (L.M. Logan), and KEEPING SERCRETS (Ophelia S. Lewis).

Enjoy these titles as part of our Reading Our World series. These books are for age groups three-to-five years and six-to-twelve years.

Adventures at **CAMP POOTIE-CHO**

- Better Together
- AACPC Good Manners ABCs
- AACPC Game & Puzzle Activity Book

- Christmas in Sanoyea
- Keeping Secrets

Meet the Campers

Join us on our adventures at Camp Pootie-Cho!

Quincy   Faaz   Gola

The Real Sapo National Park

Sapo National Park is located in Liberia, West Africa and is the country's largest protected reserve. Many endangered animals inhabit the park, which represents one of the most intact forest ecosystems in the region.

100+ Mammal species
500+ Bird Species
1000+ Flowers & Insects

Learn more at
www.camppootiecho.com